Investing for Beginners

Value Invest like a Pro, Generate Positive Cash flow and Become Financial Free

By: Christian Beach

Table of Contents

Introduction

I want to thank you and congratulate you for downloading *Investing for Beginners: How to Invest for Cash Flow*.

I was nearing the age of thirty before I started to truly consider the implications of investing for my future. Sadly, Americans often wait much longer before they start considering financial investments for their future. Nearly half of all Americans have no investments put in place at all, and another third have not saved enough for retirement. I was lucky that I discovered the importance of investing at a still relatively young age, and today I stand as a testament to how someone can make investments for both the immediate future, and for far down the line.

There lies a world of investment opportunities that can grant income both in the short, and long term. I have found that the best investments for my lifestyle are investments that provide immediate cash flow, and that is exactly what I want to teach you. The purpose of this book is to outline the virtues of investing and how to invest for multiple outcomes. Whether your ultimate purpose is retirement, savings for a house or simply trying to bolster your nest egg, I offer solutions that will guide you along your way.

If you do not start investing, then you will forever be reliant on your immediate income and the assistance of the state. Neither of these income streams are reliable in the long run, and the virtues of saving are important even when you are young and employed full time. From a six month emergency fund, to yearly appreciating fund that you use for vacation, investing has practical implications for safety and entertainment and is useful to anyone at any age.

Over the course of the following chapters you will learn about the fundamentals of investing, as well as the practicality of how to invest. Whether you have one hundred dollars or ten thousand, there are investment opportunities that you can start today that will benefit you for long into the future. It's time to put your passive money to use, to grow your savings and provide a better future for you and your family – keep reading and soon you will have a quickly growing nest egg.

Chapter 1: The Importance of Investing

Why Investing Is Important at Any Age?

When it comes to investing, the earlier you start the better off you will be. I was sadly nearly out of my twenties before I began investing, but even if you are well beyond this age, investing still holds a lot of importance. Investing offers you the ability to grow your total amount of money through passively gaining interest over time. When the virtues of investing are spelled out, the argument to become involved is quite persuasive, however the issue is that in the moment many of us choose to use money to immediate effect instead of saving and investing.

To demonstrate the importance of investing versus using your immediate cash on hand, one must merely look to a famous thought experiment: the penny problem. If I were to offer you one million dollars today, or interest gained on a penny doubling everyday for a month, which offer would you take? Without thinking too hard about the problem, many would take the more immediate money of one million dollars. If you were to go with option one, instead of taking the interest accruing option, you would end up with nearly four and a half million dollars less than if you had taken the second option.

While a penny doubling every day might not seem like a great way to accrue a lot of interest, the moment you begin to break down the problem and look at the numbers, you begin to see that is by far the more profitable option. The key is that the penny accrues interest exponentially, so that while at day two you may only have two cents, by day eight you have $1.28. By day twenty you still have not earned as much as the initial million dollars, with only $5,242.88

accruing, but by day thirty the entire pool will have grown to $5,368,709.12. There are two important lessons I want you to gain from this example: one, interest is not intuitive to humans, meaning it is hard to grasp how quickly money can grow unless we plan out the math and show the outcome. Two, the true *cost* of not receiving the million dollars up front was waiting thirty days to gain far more money. This is a key principle to investing, as what you will be trading to gain income quickly is merely the time that you are apart from your money. While you did not have one million dollars that you could use for thirty dollars, you ended up with far more money at the end of the month.

There are two last aspects of this example that are very important: what could you have done in those thirty days with one million dollars, and what is your tax obligation? In later chapters you will see that it is not always wise to hold a position in an investment if there are other opportunities to see your money rise. In the penny example, it is doubtful that you could have quintupled your money within thirty days, however there are plenty of real world scenarios where you would have been able to earn more on the initial up front cash versus leaving money in an interest bearing account. The million dollars as up front cash could have been invested to gain interest much faster than the base amount if you had left it in the account. You must also consider what your tax liability is on either sum of money. Right now the disparity between the accounts is four and a half million dollars, where you earn much more by keeping a penny in the savings account. Suppose that the disparity was far less, something on the order of just $50,000. In this case, the million dollars upfront is far more tempting, as you are gaining marginally more compared to the original scenario presented. What this does not take into account is the tax liability on the cash gained immediately versus what you would have earned within thirty days. In general the faster that you realize profit from an investment, the more costly the tax liability.

The longer you wait, the lower the tax liability. This means that you might gain far more than 50k if you held onto the investment for thirty days, not because the sum of money is much larger to begin with, but because the tax rate is far more favorable. This is a microcosm example, and for short difference in time of only thirty days, the actual tax liability is likely to be the same, but for longer stretches of time there are stark differences.

Compound Interest

You should know quite well that if someone offers you a deal to double a penny for thirty days you should certainly take it, but in the real world investing is much more difficult. You will not find these incredible opportunities so easily. However the penny example demonstrates an important aspect of investing, and one that makes it possible for your money to earn interest faster, compound interest. Compound interest allows for interest to be gained on interest that you have already accrued. The definition might seem complicated, but the concept is quite simple. In the penny example above, you can see how compound interest works, although in unrealistic scenario. The interest that is gained on the penny is doubled every day, and the new sum is the one that is doubling, allowing for the money to grow at such an exponential rate. In real terms, we have to look to a much more tame example.

Imagine that you had one hundred dollars appreciating at one percent interest, and this this is compounded four times a year. You would assume that the interest you would earn at the end of one year to be one dollar, or just one percent of your base investment, but this is not entirely accurate. It is compounding, and being added at four times per year, so after three months you have earned $0.25, or one quarter of that one percent interest. What's of note is that this small sum is added back into the base investment so that when the next interest period comes about, another three months, you are earning interest on $100.25 and not just $100. At the end of the first year this has essentially happened four times. After quarter one, you have earned $100.25, quarter two $100.50, quarter three $100.76, and quarter four $101.02. These numbers are not far off the one percent interest that you may have been originally expecting, but you can see that since the interest is compounding, you are on earning more just one quarter of one percent. Since the interest is being counted in the new sum, you are earning interest at a much faster rate. In this example, with very modest numbers, this only equals a difference of two cents, but with larger sums of money, and greater interest rates, this number can grow very quickly.

In addition, there is a separate idea of compound interest, and that is taking the interest from one investment and carrying it over to another. This is not as institutionalized as compound interest once per quarter, and is left up to the individual to work out the details. You can see though that if you were to keep track of all of the interest that you accumulated, and moved this interest to different investment ventures, your interest would grow at an accelerated rate. It is this idea of compound interest, and always using the interest gained from old investments to carry over to new interest that you can also start to see the importance of starting to invest as soon as you can. The longer you invest, regardless of the total quantity of your investments, the better off you will be. The principle of interest accruing on top of interest is simply too powerful to ignore.

Why You Have to Invest, Even When It Is a Financial Strain

Compound interest should be a fairly compelling argument for why it is to your advantage to start saving as soon as possible, however I know how difficult investing can seem when you are under financial strain. Just a few short years ago I would have had difficulty making any sort of investments in my future. I was working a moderately paying job in a very expensive city; between rent, food and travel I was consuming so much of my paycheck that investing didn't seem worth the time. This is a common mentality, and one that I understand, but it is also a mentality that will hurt you. You must start saving and investing as soon as you can, as even miniscule amounts of your salary invested will equal big gains in the long run.

Let's work with an example of a model American. Picture a man or woman, working thirty-five to forty hours a week in a grocery store. They are nearing forty years old and make around six hundred dollars a week. This means they make approximately thirty thousand dollars a year. Ignoring taxes for a moment, you know that this is not a very large sum of money. The individual that you are picturing is also middle aged, meaning that they likely have family obligations that eat into their paycheck a fairly great deal. What if this person could save just ten dollars each week, and at the end of the year used those savings to start making investments? At the end of the first year they will have saved just $520, but an investment of this size can easily earn three to four percent interest with the guidance for small capital investing in chapter two. After two years, this individual would have $1060.80, where $20.80 came from accruing interest made on the initial $520, and $520 is added as additional savings in year two. After the third year, this individual now has $1623.24, where around $63 came from interest on the first two years of savings. We can see that very quickly the interest has moved from growing at just $20 per year to over $60 per year, an increase of three times even though the interest rate hasn't changed. After year four they will have earned $2208.17; year five, $2816.50; year six, $3449.16. Six years, ten dollars a week and working with compound interest and this individual has now saved over ten percent of their yearly salary.

If saving such a small sum each week, as ten dollars is quite easy to do, can equal such a large nest egg in just a few years, imagine if you saved twenty, thirty or more dollars per week. Imagine if they had started saving at age twenty or thirty, instead of age forty. Regardless of your age, and regardless of your ability to save and invest, you must always put away money, no matter how much, so that you can reap the rewards of interest – by merely exchanging time and small savings you can build a sizable nest egg in just a few years.

Chapter 2: Investing for Cash Flow

The Types of Investments

I want you to start making cash right away from your starting investments. I realize that you are a beginner and that you likely don't have much money to invest, and that right now the virtues of investing are merely theoretical. If I can have you earn interest that you can realize as cash in hand within just a year, I think that you will have even more reason to invest. For myself personally, this was the turning point, when I started to realize that investing didn't just mean saving for the future. It meant that I would reap the rewards within just a few weeks, months or years. I didn't have to wait forever to see the benefits of my efforts and you won't have to wait either.

In this chapter you will find investments that provide the fastest accruing interest, where you can see your investment grow right in front of your eyes. Additionally, these investments have very clear cash out points where you will be able to realize your cash in hand at a clear point that you will designate. I have broken these investments into conventional and unconventional investments. Conventional investments will take longer to pay off, have a higher starting requirement but also gain large sums of interest. Unconventional investments will require more hands on time to monitor, but you will start to see interest in your hands in as little as thirty days. For best results, I would invest in both types of investments, but if you are starting with a small sum, try the unconventional investments to get greater interest and work your way into greater interest bearing conventional ventures.

A Quick Word on Saving

In chapter one you saw how at just four percent interest per year, an individual could quickly grow the size of their nest egg. What was needed for this to work however was savings. Remember that the greater your starting investment, the greater the interest that will grow. As you are just starting out, you can't just rely on the interest to grow your account, you will to have as large of an investment as possible to grow interest as fast as possible. To speed up the interest that you are gaining, I suggest that you save some of your money in very traditional ways, meaning just putting aside some money each and every week from your salary. Use this money every few months, or at the end of each year to make large investments where you will benefit from the interest. Once you have an account of a suitable size, you will find that the interest you are gaining is much greater than just saving a few dollars each week, but to get to this point you will want to work on saving up front.

Conventional Investments

Dividend Stocks

I love General Motors. I don't quite love their cars, and I've never owned a GM vehicle, but I am absolutely enthralled by the company. They pay dividend interest of over four percent last year. This is one of the main strategies for making investments; working with companies in the stock market that pay dividend interest. This is interest that is paid out to investors in a company, and the only requirement that you need to have for earning this interest is to be a shareholder. For each share of GM stock that you own, you will get paid a dividend interest for owning those shares. In this case, the interest that is gained is quite large at over four percent. The key to working with dividend interest is to understand that your base investment is a two to three year investment, and that the amount of money that you can make from your investment is directly proportional to how many shares of a company that you own. Don't let the long time requirement worry you too much; you will be earning dividend interest *at least* once a year. There are two very important aspects to dividend interest that I need to mention: one, although this is the stock market, this is not a very risky investment. Two, you are earning interest on the shares of the company that you own, but by owning shares you are gaining access to a wholly separate type of investment, the shares themselves.

The concept of dividends is simple, but many Americans can have a difficult time explaining exactly what they are and how they function. When you make an investment in a company on the stock market, they want to make sure that you hold onto your shares of stock. As the market becomes tight for buying new shares of the company, the company might have the potential to split their stock, create shares and increase the total value in the company. This is because the total value of the company is technically equivalent to their market capitalization, which is a function of the stock price, multiplied by the total number of shares sold in a company. The key for the company is to make sure that investors are happy. There are two basic ways of doing this, and they play into each other quite nicely for investors. The first way is that they simply increase the value of the company, driving up demand for their stock and increasing their stock price. A company like Apple is quite good at this, as just a few years ago their actual dividends were quite low, however they held onto investors because the stock was climbing so quickly. An investor would get involved in the stock merely to sell it at a later date, knowing that the stock was likely to climb in value. Google in the early to mid 2000s also did not have to pay out dividends frequently either. Their company was growing at such an electric rate that the growth in the value of the stock was enough to lure investors. Most companies do not have the luxury of having a stock grow very quickly, or at least quickly enough to lure an ever increasing number of investors.

For large established companies, ones that have steady profits but little in terms of revolutionizing technology and markets like Apple and Google, they have to take a different approach to holding onto investors. They use dividends as an incentive for investors to hold onto their stock. Dividends will pay out some amount of money per share, meaning that the more holdings an investor has in a company, the greater the size of their dividends. This incentives investors to take as large as a position as possible to earn even more immediate income from the dividends. To give you an idea of how much these dividends pay, this is one of the key investments that trusts use. Trusts want to use very low risk investments that have some degree of certitude that they will be able to earn interest on whatever the investment. By working with dividend stocks, or rather stocks that are well known to pay dividends to share holders, trusts can have assurance in the security of their investments.

The two ways that companies lure investors to hold onto their stock are not mutually exclusive, and for us as investors, both aspects can pay out nicely. If you become invested in a dividend stock like GM or American Airlines Group, you will be earning income every three months to a year depending on how the company pays out dividends. In addition, you are also sitting on a windfall of potential income from the sale of the stock. In general, you can expect that the stock of a company will go up over a long enough period of time. This means that you are earning interest every single year through dividends, but at the end of a few years you can also sell the base investment that you made, earning you in one fell swoop a great deal of interest on your investment.

Getting invested in the stock market may seem like a scary idea to new investors, but the truth is that we are making long term investments that are very secure. There is a general attitude towards the stock market for those that have not had many personal investments that it is the wild west of investments, that fortunes are gained and lost in mere days. The truth is that the stock market is far more stable than many people give it credit for, and that over time you can expect the whole market to gain value. Just in the last fifteen years the Dow Jones has more than doubled in total value, and this is through the great recession and financial crisis of 2008 and 2009. The key to making secure investments in the stock market is to work with well known and stable companies, and for added reassurance work with ones that have dividend payments so that you can start earning right away. Investing in the stock market where you invest and just sit back is the best way to make stable income – investments where you have to constantly monitor the stock like a day trader; these are the more risky investments where you probably get your perspective of the stock market being a very risky endeavor.

There are only two real downsides to this investment. One is that to earn lots of immediate cash you nee to own a sizeable number of shares of a company. More specifically, I would expect that you would earn about $300 every three months on a $5,000 stake in the market, give or take. Even if you can't buy in for many shares, remember that you can sell those shares later, making the investment more than just the immediate cash from the dividend payments. The second problem is that while in the long run the market will go up, there are at times financial crises of different sizes. This would change both the dividend payments received and your ability to earn interest on stocks sold. If this happens, the best possible strategy to take is to stick with the market and wait it out. The odds of this happening are low, but it is a risk to be aware of.

Real Estate

For a short period of time after the housing crisis of 2008, there was talk about how it possibly made more sense to rent an apartment or home than to buy one. Today, this is no longer true. In most cities and towns in America, it makes far more sense to buy where you are going to live than to simply rent. There are of course special circumstance where this isn't true; those that wish to move for example, but for the vast majority of Americans owning a home simply makes sense. Even if you do not live in that home, the interest that appreciates on a home is some of the largest that you can make for any investment. The utility of a home comes from begin able to live there, but also due to the large amount of money that is gained when selling a property. This makes for a multiyear investment, but within just five years, you could literally double your money on properties in certain parts of the country. For example, looking at the most popular cities where new residents are moving in at the fastest rates, you can see that houses are truly appreciating at rates of up to ten to twenty percent per year. Austin, Texas and San Francisco fall into these cites where after a couple of years you can make a tremendous amount of profit. The key is that these cites are now getting prohibitively expensive, making it difficult to buy a home in the present day climate. For most Americans, they would be better off simply buying a home in the area where they live, and selling this after five to ten years, depending on whether or not they are using it. Still, there is hope if you are wishing to make a lot of money very quickly by buying into a city where they have seen massive growth the last few years but the prices for houses are still relatively modest. I look to cities like Saint Louis and Minneapolis, as they have fast growing populations but are currently ripe with housing.

A home does not need to be multiyear investment to see any type of interest accruing on your home. There is a simple an easy way to start seeing cash from your investment; renting a property that you purchase. This is more in depth than merely buying a property and selling it at a later date. You become an active partner in ensuring that your home is bringing in money, but what you are doing is also providing an additional income stream for your home. By renting out a home that you purchase you are essentially able to sell the home at a later date for a large sum, but also collect monthly payments from tenants in your properties. This is not going to be an option that works for everyone, but as a large investment that starts to pay back immediately, it can certainly work for many investors.

Additionally, there is value in more than just a house or apartment. The land itself is often quite valuable, and will grow in value over time. What's nice about this is that the cost of investment is far less than a home, and your obligation to build on any land purchased is zero, so you can hold onto the deed and sell it at a later date. I know of a few investors that got involved in this in parts of Florida. They would buy empty lots and hold onto them for a few years, paying property tax on the land, and mostly losing money, until they got a chance to sell the property to either someone. These sales would come from individuals who wanted to build a home on it, or far more lucrative, a company wanting to build a housing complex. This is a more risky investment as it is not always as clear cut that your land will be valuable in the future. At the same time the cost to entry is far cheaper and it is not as though you cannot make an accurate assessment of what land in your area will be valuable in the future. Looking into empty lots, which many consider undesirable, and making a purchase is a great way to provide future income when someone comes to you wanting to buy that land. The only risk is the length of time till the land increases in value.

Going into real estate yourself is very expensive, but there is a way to mitigate this cost by turning to a real estate investment trust. These are groups of people that pool their money together to buy real estate. Members typically either vote on a property, or there is a central manger that decides the purchases. These groups make money much the same way an individual would profit from a property. A property is bought and then sold at a later date, with the profits being split between all the investors.

This is a great way to make interest from property investments without having to be the sole investor in a project. It also opens up some neat options that you may not have access to without a trust. For one, you have access to a set of skills that all of your fellow trust members have. While the responsibility of picking out a property that will gain in value is can be daunting for the individual, having a group work on this task together can lead to improved results. You have a pool of information far larger than what you posses individually, leading to better picks. Second, the size of the property and therefore the interest can increase quite a bit. You are able to buy properties in already desirable parts of town; parts of your area where you know demand is going to increase in the very near future. This allows you to make a shorter time investment but still gain a great deal of interest. Third, and perhaps the most important feature real estate trust offer, the group as a whole can finance the improvement of a property. This is an essential aspect of real estate investment trusts that is much harder for the individual to perform. A group will buy a property that needs work and maintenance to be sellable. They will then either hire a crew to fix the property, or do it themselves. A real estate trust can often have twenty plus members, and many of those often specialize in fixing up properties. They simply join the trust to gain access to a greater pool of capital. It is not too uncommon to have these members of the trust take a slightly larger cut of the profits since they put in more effort, but the profit that is made from a fixed up home should not be understated. There are entire businesses that operate on this model, and while it is on a smaller scale with a real estate trust, it is still an incredible opportunity to earn interest on your investment.

Finally, a real estate group is very apt at collecting rent from tenants if they choose to rent out properties. With ten to twenty people working together, the idea of maintaining a few properties that are rented out to tenants becomes much easier. In a way it is almost like running a business except on a much smaller scale. These groups tend to have only a few tenants at most, because at a certain point these trusts would need to hire outside help, and that would cut into the profits of the trust. This is a great way to earn immediate interest on your investment, and have the help to work through the difficulties of renting out properties. In addition, like other aspects of the real estate trust, you gain access to the knowledge and knowhow of everyone within the trust, making this whole venture much easier.

I become involved in a real estate trust in my area about a year ago, and it has proved to be one of the smartest investments that I have ever made. The real estate trust paid back 150% of my initial investment in a year, something that is very hard to reach with other investments. I want to say that you cannot expect this type of success from most real estate trusts, and that our market was at a particular advantage due to an influx of business in our area. There are many individuals and families looking for homes, and our trust has enough resources to buy and sell homes fairly quickly, as well as renting two properties. Right now our focus is on buying a property, doing minimal work to fix it up, and then selling it a few months later. For example, last spring we purchased a home for $250k. We put in around another ten thousand dollars in redoing one of the bathrooms, fixing the tile in the kitchen and adding French doors to the back of the house. Honestly, we probably overpaid for the work, but no one in my trust is quite handy or able to do this type of work easily – we needed to hire outside contractors, who are already quite busy with the influx of requests in our area. This home ended up selling for $370k around nine months after we purchased it. It is hard to find an investment that will pay this much back, and as far as I know I believe this is the most successful investment that our trust has ever made, but it goes to show what can happen when a property is purchased and a little bit of work is put in. In total we made around $90k after taxes; this net me personally $5,200.

To get involved in a real estate trust in your area is going to be highly dependent on the social circles you are involved with, how large your town or city is and the amount of capital you have to offer for this venture. Our trust started as a community investment fund that turned to specialize in housing and development. To join our trust you need at least ten thousand dollars, which is a steep investment for many. The benefits of a trust far outweigh the costs however, and I would suggest this method of investment to anyone seeking to make money from real estate. The money is lucrative enough that I would even suggest starting your own trust if you have the ability. Demonstrating to others the value of pooling your money together for real estate is not that difficult of a pitch, as you can simply point to the increasing home values in your area. Also the total time commitment for this type of venture is relatively low, making it an ideal investment that will take up a very minimal amount of your time.

Unconventional Investments

Peer-to-Peer Lending

If you are just starting out investing, then I suggest you head online and look at peer-to-peer lending. This is not a venture that is going to make you immediately rich, but you will start to see interest on your investment within just thirty days. The key to this style of investing is that you are making a one to one transaction with someone online. This can be someone in the United States or someone abroad that needs between five hundred and one thousand dollars of investment. Sometimes they need even less money, however the interest rates on small payments are very low. The main issue with this service is two fold; one there is no enforcement to make sure that you get paid, instead relying on a reputation system. And two, many of these sites were set up to be virtuous, meaning that the total interest collected is relatively low for the service you offer. That being said, do not dismiss to peer-to-peer lending right away. This was an investment where I was able to clear one thousand dollars of interest in just a little over six months. It was in fact one of the first investments that I participated in.

The way that this system works is that you are lending money directly to an individual, typically paid through PayPal. This money can be used for any number of things, from a mortgage payment, to fixing a car to paying for a wedding. In many cases it is used to finance an emergency, and an individual will turn to a peer-to-peer lending service because they are either in a line of work that does not allow them to receive a payday loan (no pay stub from their place of employment), or they use the online service first because the rates of payday loans are loosely regulated and very expensive. You can typically expect interest of around ten percent for thirty days, so on a five hundred dollar loan you will earn fifty dollars within thirty days. This might seem like a very small amount to gain for risking losing five hundred dollars, but a ten percent return in thirty days is actually very good. There are also numerous systems in place to mitigate the chance of not being paid back at all.

For example, people requesting money have a reputation system attached to them, so you can choose to only lend to those that have paid because all previous loans. This reduces quite bit of the inherit risk of this system, and allows you to make more secure investments in peer-to-peer lending. The more secure the investment, the lower the amount of interest that you can collect; however the interest rates will still be quite favorable to lenders. The lowest interest rates that I have ever seen were around five to seven percent, and this was exceedingly rare. Using this system for myself, I was able to earn about $1000 within about eight months. Of all of my investments, every single person I lent to paid me back within the allotted time. The average rate of interest was around ten percent, which means that I loaned about ten thousand dollars out over eight months. What's important to note is that I in no way started with ten thousand dollars, but as I started to see more and more interest from the payments I was collecting, I became more invested in this venture. I would suggest this as a great way to go if you are just starting out as an investor, and do not have the capital to get invested in the larger investment opportunities above. It will be a fairly length road till you are earning a great deal of income from interest, but as you practice this method you can lend more and more money over time, increasing the amount that you make from interest. Like with all things investing, we start small and build up our pile of money, opening up additional opportunities for investments.

Investing in a Local Business

I was reading a blog just last year about getting invested in local businesses. I figured this was an article about how large companies are becoming invested in local businesses, but quite to the contrary it was about how everyday people are opening up lines of communication with local businesses and offering them support. This is especially true with new businesses as they are expanding to reach their minimum number of customers they need to be sustainable. For example, I found that if you invest in a local business in Philadelphia, you stand to earn a great deal of interest. This is because in the city of Philadelphia it is extremely difficult to get a license to serve liquor. This is usually an issue of not having the fund to hire the right people to get this license. If individuals would help fund a restaurant to get a liquor license, they would get some portion of all of the proceeds from the profits made off the sale of alcoholic beverages.

In my own city we do not have such strict regulations to get a liquor license, and nearly all restaurants are able to serve alcohol if they want to. I figured that there was no place for this investment opportunity in my own city, but I also knew that there was no harm in asking around. What I found was that multiple restaurants and retail stores were seeking investors, and are extremely interested because this is a type of cash investment that goes outside of banks. Loans for businesses that I found tended to be on a scale between one thousand and ten thousand dollars, making some of these investments quite large. I decided to get invested in two businesses: one was a local sporting goods store and the other was a restaurant. I invested one thousand dollars in the sporting goods store and two thousand in the restaurant.

With my money, both of these business were able to expand. It is worth noting that the owners of these stores were also quite invested, but they used my investment to supplement the costs for making improvements to these stores. For the sporting goods store, they simply used the money to front the payment of new sporting goods for fencing. I thought this was odd until I found out the local high school had recently started a fencing team – the problem was that there was no where to buy the equipment. I'm not sure on the total cost of the equipment that was purchased through my local business, but I know that it was more than the one thousand dollars I lent them. Over the course of the following three months, I earned $220 on this investment, plus the base investment that I received back. Twenty-two percent interest on a one thousand dollar investment for three months without any monitoring is not bad at all, but the limitations to making this investment were that I had to reach out the business. I never would have found this opportunity if I didn't ask around my city and find out that this business was in need of investors. I believe this is the reason that I found myself in this position, as this investment seemed like such a good idea that I can't believe others hadn't taken the owner up on the investment. The truth is that the owner never asked any individuals for investments because they never thought that anyone would be willing to help them; they figured they would have to go to a bank. In this situation, everyone wins, and if I ever have kids I know that we'll get a great price on sporting equipment at a store that I was happy to invest in.

The second investment in the restaurant turned out to be an even better deal. This was an investment that I too was puzzled why the restaurant owner hadn't been able to collect money from other customers. Just like with the sporting goods store, the owner of the restaurant felt it inappropriate to seek investment from patrons. When I came to ask the owner if he would take my investment money, provided he told me exactly what he was going to use it for, he was simply shocked. He told me that the restaurant would be using the money to build a deck in the back so that they could have more tables, expanding the amount of money they could make per hour, and also make the restaurant more desirable by having outside seating. I was convinced and over the next six months I earned my money back plus an additional $450 in interest, or 22.5% interest on a six-month investment. Again, it is hard to see returns like this in many markets. In addition I find that I often have a smaller bill at that restaurant when I dine there than I really should; the owner typically will give me a complimentary drink or deduct the cost of a side dish. I don't know what the total cash value of this investment is overall, but the point is that it paid back 22.5% in six moths, plus offered additional perks.

I highly suggest that you go down this avenue if have at least one thousand dollars to invest in a business venture. With the two stores that I invested in, I went with clear cut investments and I knew what they would be used for. I am not an expert at sporting goods, nor have I ever owned a restaurant, but even to most reasonable people what these businesses owners were trying to do was quite clear; simply expand their businesses. To get started with this type of unconventional investment, reach out to local businesses in your area. It is as simple as asking if they are open to investment. I'm sure you will find some store owners are confused by your offer, but if you make it clear what you are offering, some support to improve their business in exchange for interest and a return on investment, you should be able to find one or two businesses that will be interested in your support.

Chapter 3: Invest Like the Pros

The Pro Investor

The professional investor does not monitor their investments everyday. In fact they monitor their investments once every quarter or once every six months. That is because the pro investor has made investments that are slow and steady, paying interest at regular intervals and are safe enough investments that the investor does not have to worry about pulling out at the right time. Many of these investments are on a huge scale, where the rich can live off of just three percent interest per year. To grasp this idea, look at the way that a trust fund works, as this is emblematic of the pro investor.

A trust fund is a pool of money that is handled by professional investors to make steady interest in safe investments. A trust fund is not trying to maximize returns, because that is not how a professional investor thinks. They are rather acting on trying to maximize funds within a certain allotment of risk. As long as they can make steady returns, that is the most important aspect. What allows them to be so conservative in their investments is the pool of money that they are working with, and the rules about how this money is to be handed out. A trust works by keeping a large amount of money in a fund for investments, and only hands out the accumulated interest to the trustees. There are exceptions and trusts can be set up in a number of different ways, but if you've seen a trust that has been in existence for one hundred years, for scholarships for example, this is a trust that only finances trustees with interest. If you look at a university's endowment, you can see how a one percent return on a billion dollars becomes quite significant. One percent of one billion dollars is ten million dollars - not an insignificant sum of money. Replicating these types of investments on a scale tuned to our level of investment is a little more tricky, but that doesn't mean that trusts and safe investments are not available to us.

We can indeed have the same style of investments as the very rich, and I highly suggest that you keep a least one of the following investment opportunities in mind. These are investments that you will need to keep adding money to, and for each dollar that you add you will earn more and more interest. While you may never get up to a billion dollars on your base investment, the greater the amount you enter the greater your returns. For my own part, this is where all of my investment returns go. I take the money that I make from other investments and split them into two of the three following funds (you will see why I don't participate in one fund). As each fund grows, so do my returns far down the line. What's nice about these funds is that in addition to being very safe, they are also highly favorable for taxes. These long term investments are taxed at a much more favorable rate than short term investments, something that will be made clear in the next chapter.

Mimicking Their Investments

Index Funds

A few years ago Warren Buffett made a bet against managers of a large hedge fund. The hedge fund specialized in making investments for clients, and seeing these investments grow. Warren Buffett had a different idea, that no matter how talented the investor, they could never make as much money from the stock market than if they bet on an index fund. The bet took place over ten years, and the prize was a million dollars. The prize money was mostly symbolic, as all parties involved had tens of millions, if not billions of dollars like Buffett himself. The bet symbolized an important idea though: could investors really outplay the market as a whole?

The basis of this bet was that index funds are an all around safer investment than to try and beat the average of the market. The way that an index fund works, is that the money in the fund raises proportionally to how an entire exchange is doing. For example, bet on an index fund that works with the New York Stock Exchange, and as long as the exchange is doing well as a whole, then the fund will grow. There was little debate as to whether or not the fund would appreciate in value, but would the fund really outpace one of the world's most competitive hedge funds? Astoundingly, the answer was yes, an index fund really could beat out the smartest investors in the world. By making bets on particular companies and leaving out others, investors as a whole had made a grave mistake about trying to beat the market altogether. This bet proves that no matter how smart you are, no matter how talented, an index fund will beat out the bets that you make. In addition, an index fund requires absolutely no effort to monitor. You simply hand over your money and watch it appreciate; you don't have to move around investments, and you don't have to make picks as to what companies you think will do better than the market average.

For investors on a small scale, index funds do have a few drawbacks. When you invest in an index fund, you shouldn't expect to start seeing your returns for around four to five years. This is typically how long you will want to keep your money invested. You can collect the interest at regular times, but in general you want to keep that money in the fund so that the fund can grow at a faster rate. I suggest this avenue to any investor that is fine with making a five-year investment. To truly maximize your earnings potential with an index fund, you want to invest as much money as possible. This is one of the safest investments that you can possibly make however, and leaving your money for five years in a fund is extremely low risk.

There are two primary hazards to index funds, but even one of these drawbacks can still lead to great returns for an investor. The two worries are that either the stock market has a crash that it simply cannot recover from or that the stock market takes part in a global recession where inflation outpaces the growth of the index fund. This first scenario of a global catastrophe is very unlikely, and the government has shown that it will do everything in its power to avoid a complete collapse of the global financial system. Essentially if this future comes to pass, you will have much more to worry about than just your investment fund. A large scale crash that would wipe out an index fund would likely take a sizeable portion of the US economy with it, making no investment truly safe. As for the second scenario of a recession in the economy, this is far less of a worry. In the bet that Buffett made with the hedge fund managers, he was still able to claim victor even through the great recession at the turn of the last decade. What this will mean for an ordinary investor is that they might lose some money after five years, but after ten they will have earned that back plus additional returns. Essentially while it is possible that an index fund may go down in some time interval, it will not stay down in the long run. This means that if you find that your fund has actually decreased, you can simply keep your money in the fund for longer, until it appreciates past the starting level and you start to make real returns again. The true downside then is that your money is inaccessible for a longer period of time. I would advise this method of investment to anyone with a decent size investment fund, and would caution to say that you should expect that at a minimum you won't touch the money for five years, including the interest, with the worse case scenario meaning the money is inaccessible for ten years. In either case, when you withdraw the money you will be earning a percentage of returns greater than any hedge fund. You can always collect the interest as it accrues for immediate cash flow, but this might be better done after you've given the fund a few years to grow.

Mutual Funds

After an index fund, I would recommend a mutual fund as your next go to option. A mutual fund is an organization that takes money from investors and places them in bundles of stocks that are thought to be safe investments. You read how in chapter two there are stocks that pay dividends to attract investors and keep them invested. These are the types of stocks that mutual funds invest in; stocks that will pay out at regular time periods and are also not very volatile. A mutual fund may also diversify investments outside of stocks, and also get involved in treasury bonds and even stock options. They will do whatever it takes to earn a steady return for their investors.

What's great about mutual funds is that while they might not earn as much interest in the long run as an index fund, they are essential for gaining a quick cash flow. A mutual fund will inform all of its investors at regular time periods of how their accounts are doing, and you can take out any portion of the mutual fund at any time without suffering any penalties, outside of it becoming taxable income for that year.

When I got started investing, mutual funds played a critical role in getting an early cash flow going. I created a T. Rowe Price mutual fund with just $3000, and over the course of a year I was making around $200 in returns. I would collect this interest and leave the base investment in the mutual fund. Obviously it would have been more beneficial in the long run to leave the money in the mutual fund, but that's not what this was about; it was about being able to collect immediate cash flow from my investment.

I would advise that you get involved with a mutual fund, and that you start an account with around one thousand dollars. From my own experience I would recommend T. Rowe Price. They offer a variety of different mutual funds that have different levels of expected risk, meaning you can look for lots of returns very quickly with high risk, or take a more stable position for lower returns. For my own part, I went with the middle choice of a fund that was relatively safe, but still had a decent expected return rate. You can find the mutual fund that is right for you with the expected returns that are most favorable for the risk that you want to take on; I suggest going this avenue if you want immediate income, and use an index fund if you want to invest for a longer time period.

529 College Savings Fund

A 529 account is a very particular type of investment fund. It can only be used for college education expenses, is authorized buy the Internal Revenue Service, and is managed by the individual states and the District of Columbia. I decided to include the 529 savings plan because a huge part of investing is planning for the future and to reduce some of the worry about providing for your family. College education has become quite a necessity in modern labor markets, and a college savings plan will greatly help you pay for this burden.

The 529 plans come in two types, and your state will offer both plans, or just one plan or the other. There are the pre-paid plans and the standard college savings plan. More states currently offer the college savings plan, and this is likely the type of investment that you will use if you create a 529. The difference between these two plans is that with a pre-paid account you can start paying for a particular university right now, at the cost of the university in 2017. These payments typically work by paying for each credit hour, and generally only work at state institutions. For example you could start paying for the credit hours that your child plans to use in the future at a variety of state institutions. They can then decide to go to any state institution of your choice, and these payments will carry over. If your child does not go to a state school, then you either lose the investment or suffer severe penalties to get any money out of the plan. It is also worth noting that for nearly all institutions, the pre-paid plan can only be used for college credits and not for room or board or other expenses.

The general savings plan is more open with what you can use the money for, but also does not reduce the costs as severely. This money can be used on a state school or private institution, and money paid into an account will be dispersed with a severe tax reduction when your child is ready to go to school. If you end up not having any children that attend college, you are eligible to retrieve the money but for a heavy penalty. The harshness of this penalty is variable depending on the state. This fund can also be used to fund your own education, and does not have to be used as a college or university. It can be used at a trade school for instance, or in a job retraining program.

A 529 plan has a very particular type of payoff – the education of your children. The mounting costs are worrisome though, and you can expect college tuition to only rise, as a college degree becomes more of a requisite to get a good job. Research how the 529 plan functions in your state and start an account if you know you will have children going to college. Specifically for college education, this is single handedly the best fund you can set up. Money in a 529 fund appreciates quickly and the reductions on taxes on this savings account are some of the most generous that the government offers. This is a fund that nearly all rich Americans use to send their kids to school; there is no reason why you shouldn't use it too.

Chapter 4: Your End of the Bargain

Taxes

In life, the only certainties are death and taxes. You will indeed need to pay taxes on your investments, but how investments are taxed is actually quite different than your standard income. Depending on how much you make, the state you live in and whether or not you are contractor, your current tax obligation is going to vary quite a bit. You may be able to receive the earned income tax credit, or you may have to pay taxes yourself if you are a contractor. With your investments, you should start to pay twice as much attention to your taxes because they are about to change.

For starters, there is a general rule about the way that taxes for investments work in the United States. If you hold onto an investment for a year or longer, your tax burden goes down significantly. This works through a system called the capital gains tax, which has two variants in short and long term capital gains. The system has changed over the years, and even as you are reading this book there are talks in the capital about adjusting the tax rate yet again. Currently the way that it works is that any investment in which you collect profit in less than one year gets added to your taxable income. So for example, if you make $40,000 a year and earn $5,000 in the stock market and collect it within a year, then your total taxable income becomes $45,000. This will greatly affect higher income earners than low income workers, however if you make $25,000 a year and collect $5,000 from the stock market, you can expect that you will no longer qualify for certain government assistance programs. This is something that you need to keep in mind as you cash out your investments.

Thankfully there is the long term capital gains tax, where profits from investments are taxed at a maximum of 20%, and this is only for those at the highest tiers of the tax bracket. For most readers of this book, the burden is more likely to be between 0% and 15%. If your tax bracket is in the 0% to 15%, then long term capital gains is taxed at zero dollars. For example if you make $25,000 a year, you can expect that your taxes on a $5,000 profit from selling stocks is going to be 0%. This is a huge differentiator in your tax burden, and it always makes sense to keep investments tied up for a full year to avoid the tax burden of short term capital gains. Above being taxed at 0% for many Americans, it also reduces their income bracket than if they had collected profits within the first year. The fact that your overall taxes would increase and that you might lose some government assistance is a big deal, making the long term capital gains tax all the more appealing.

In addition to wanting to keep your investments for a year or longer, you will also want to consider your possible deductions for your investments. For example, if one or more of your investments proves to not be profitable, then you are able to carry that tax over to increase your maximum deduction. This is best practiced with an accountant, but the basic idea is that until your investments become profitable, any losses realized or not become deductions that you can enact on your taxes. You can carry over these deductions for a number of years too, so even if other investments make you income but one does not, the negative investment will be carried over as deductions on your tax forms as long as it does not turn into a profit.

In chapter two you learned about some unconventional investments. These investments were much more personable and did not involve very large institutions. Remember that these are still investments that you need to declare on your tax returns, including investments that you make in local businesses. The reason I mention this here is that there needs to be consistency in tax forms. For example, if you find out that one of your investment partners in a real estate trust is not going to declare income, you need to get them on board with paying the right amount of taxes, or else you and your partner open yourself up to an audit. The same is true with investing in a restaurant or local business; make sure that there is consistency in tax returns and all parties involved in an investment are reporting their taxes accurately.

Time Requirements

The amount of time that you have to dedicate to investing is not very much, and depending on the investments that you make, you may find that you are hardly monitoring your investments at all. If you decide to go with the strategies in chapter two, namely the conventional investments, you can expect there to be some upfront work to be done to find suitable investments, but for the investments to grow naturally after your initial efforts. For example if you want to become involved in a dividend stock, you must merely research what stocks are paying dividends and how frequently, and maybe monitor your investment once a month, ensuring that it is not depreciating.

The unconventional investments in chapter two require more effort, but these are mostly investments about making personal contact with others. Whether that contact is to arrange a real estate trust, or simply to get involved in a local business, your investment will need more monitoring but only to the degree that you trust your investment partners. Even when investing in a local business, your partner in this case is the owner of the store, and based on your level of trust you will need to check up on the business every so often. If you do not know the owner very well, you will want to create a rapport so that you can check on your investment frequently and with ease.

Where to Start?

Chapter two offers the best strategies for investors that are just starting out. These are methods that you can use to earn relatively fast returns and are fairly low cost to start. I truly believe that it doesn't matter where you start, but that what is going to determine your starting position is how much capital you are starting with. Even the more advanced strategies in chapter three can prove to be immediately beneficial. Work within the framework of the starting investment that you have, and you will do fine. Note that all of the investments in this book are relatively safe and do not require lots of active monitoring. You can simply investment, sit back and collect your returns.

Chapter 5: The Value Investor Mindset

The Value Investor: Warren Buffett

Warren Buffett is one of the richest people in the world, and yet he lives a very modest life. He has lived in the same home for decades, doesn't own a fleet of expensive cars and doesn't spend his money on large items like yachts; a staple purchase for billionaires. Warren Buffett advocates value stocks, or stocks that are worth more or less than they appear. This is an investment strategy that has long term implications, and is one of the top tier strategies for maximizing your returns. It is also one of the most difficult to practice, as it requires a deep understanding of markets and the mindset of other investors that seek short term gains. Thankfully, by listening to Warren's words, we can at least adopt some of the clear strengths of value investments.

The basic premise behind value investments is that you are buying into a company that is worth more than the current trading value. Conversely, you can also short sell a company that you believe is trading for too high a value. Warren has engaged in both activities, but he's better known for finding companies that are likely to increase in value over time. To understand how the market can undervalue or overvalue companies, you must merely look at how the market reacts to news. For example, three years ago when Dell announced a series of new computers in their product line, investors jumped on Dell stock. They saw this as a great opportunity to ride an upturn in investment. Traders like Warren were a little more dubious about Dell. They saw this as a company that had just sacrificed long term value for short term gain. Their product line was not innovating, but rather just offering more products due to the customization of essentially the same old product. Shortly after the rally around Dell stock, investors began to realize that it had been overvalued and the stock fell into a decline. An investor could have made money from this change by short selling the stock – this is a rather high level strategy and I wouldn't recommend it for beginners, but value trading works the other way just as often.

During the great recession many companies were undervalued, and investors like Buffett decided to bet against the market and pick up this stock. These companies include GM, who now pays out some of the highest dividends on any exchange. For the beginning investor, this is where you have to focus; what is currently being traded at a lower value than it really should. It is not an easy thing to practice, so we're going to need a little help.

Following Warren

Buffett bets on the intrinsic value of a stock being greater than the current trading value. I can't identify these stocks very well, but I don't have to. I must merely look at the many comments that Buffett puts out regularly and invest in those commodities. For example, the only reason that I invested in GM stock to get dividends was based on the advice of Warren Buffett. His musing about the stock market is free information for where to find value in investments. Identifying these picks by yourself requires digging deep into the financials of a company, and seeing that they are undervalued based on their current asset list. For normal investors, this is a lot of time, and also something that you need to have special training for. If you merely follow the advice of value investors, investors with proven track records like Buffett, you can trade like a professional value trader. These are longer term investments, even those that pay dividends several times a year, but if you have the ability to invest in the value stocks that Buffett recommends, I suggest you do so. So far he has proven to provide invaluable advice that has only seen my returns grow over the years.

Conclusion

Thank you again for downloading *Investing for Beginners: How to Invest for Cash Flow.*

You now know the strategies necessary to make great returns through both short and long term investments. You are aware of the tax burden, and how professional traders make money in the markets. You know the time commitment is low, and that all it takes to get started is to start investing. You are also ware of the strong virtues of investing, and that you should start as soon as you can. Even if saving and investing is difficult for you right now, the payoff is so large that it is well worth your time to start investing.

Your next step is to set up your investment pool and find an investment that meets your requirements for earning interest and is suitable for how much money you are starting with. My major suggestion is to start with dividend stocks and peer-to-peer lending. Peer-to-peer lending will start earning you interest within thirty days, and dividend stocks will provide checks throughout the year. For a list of great dividend stocks, just refer to the suggestions by Warren Buffett; the value investor that this book bases its ideals on. The investments that I have made in the stock market are all based on Warren's advice, and they have proved to be immensely profitable in the few short years since I started investing.

Lastly, remember the tax burden and the cost of seeking immediate returns versus holding your investment for a year. This is a huge issue for those on the lower tiers of the income ladder, and those that have government assistance. You must note that any profit claimed within a year of investing must be listed as income on your current tax returns. This will change the amount of taxable income and may disqualify you for certain benefits. Always verify by either checking online or with a professional accountant whether or not it makes more financial sense for you to claim for the short term capital gains tax. Early on, it was far wiser to pay the steeper tax penalty, abut as my finances grew, it became clear that the long term capital gains tax was far more beneficial.

Finally if you enjoyed this book, it would be much appreciated if you could leave a review on Amazon. The best way for this book to make its way into the hands of more readers is through truthful reviews about this work. Please write what you liked about this book and what could be improved upon. Any and all feedback is helpful as I continue to serve the needs of my readership.

Thank you and good luck!

BONUS: Preview of my Personal Finance Book, chapter 6

The book includes:

Chapter 6: Patience – Becoming Wealthy Does Not Happen Overnight

In the last two chapters, we looked at some of the habits wealthy people have compared to the habits that poor people have. This is not to imply that you can simply decide to change your habits and tomorrow you are going to wake up wealthy. It is going to take a lot more time and patience than that. It is also going to take a lot of hard work and commitment. However, it is not impossible.

Patience is easily one of the most important factors when it comes to money. While patience isn't a guarantee of success, it does dramatically increase your odds of success. Patience is also one of the hardest traits to learn. Especially since we live in a culture of now. We tend to look for instant gratification, and we are constantly bombarded by messages that are trying to convince us that this is okay. The messages we are seeing are telling us to buy now, to spend now, and to get what we want right now.

When you buy something now, instead of waiting until you can truly afford it, you cost yourself more money. This is because you are likely relying on credit to purchase the item that you want right now. Patience is the key to overcoming this.

Below we are going to look at a few of the ways patience is going to help you achieve your financial goals.

Patience Lets Your Money Grow – The longer you can hold onto your money, the more of it you are going to have. When you leave a pool of money alone, it can compound interest and grow before your eyes. This is going to allow you to afford more in the future, by being patient now.

Patience Teaches Your Discipline – When you find something that you want to have now, wait thirty days before you buy it. In many cases, you are going to find that you can live without the item that seemed so urgent just a few weeks ago. You are going to feel better about yourself because you were able to exercise discipline and aren't going to have buyer's remorse over the product you bought. Patience is going to help you to prevent mistakes from happening.

Patience Allows You To Seize Opportunities – By having the patience to wait instead of buying the item you want right now, you are going to be able to spend time comparison shopping and researching cheaper alternatives. If you aren't in a rush for an item, you can practice predatory shopping. Predatory shopping means that you watch and wait for bargains and markdowns which allow you to save even more money.

Patience Lets You Discover What's Important – As you age and mature, your values are going to change. If you are willing to wait, you are going to learn more about yourself and what is truly important to you. Patience is going to help you practice conscious spending and keep you from buying something that you aren't going to care to have in a few months.

Patience Keeps You Sane – Being patient means that you aren't going to care about having to keep up with other people on having what is new. It means that you are not going to give into fads and trends. You are going to be willing to buy last year's model of a product and keep it until it dies. It means you aren't going to care about what your neighbors have, and you are going to live a quiet and content life.

Being patient is going to lead you to be happier and lead you to wealth. It is hard to be patient when you are always watching TV, listening to the radio and using the internet.

Our society doesn't believe in or encourage, patience. Our society is all about now and instant gratification. This is where practicing more of the habits that wealthy people practice is going to help you achieve your goals.

Another advantage of being patient is that you are going to be able to stay committed to your goals. If you aren't able to exercise patience you are going to have a hard time making a goal and seeing it through to the end. This means that when you make a goal to create and stick to a budget, which we are going to cover in the next chapter, you aren't going to have the patience to stick to the budget you created and followed it.